Fall
BULLETIN
BOARDS
for Sunday School

MW01011796

Publisher .... *Arthur L. Miley*

Author .... *Carolyn Passig Jensen*

Art Director .... *Debbie Birch*

Cover Design .... *Gary Zupkas*

Production Director .... *Barbara Bucher*

Production Assistant .... *Valerie Fetrow*

Illustrator .... *Fran Kizer*

Production Artist .... *Nelson Beltran*

Proofreader .... *Barbara Bucher*

Rainbow Publishers

Copyright © 1997 • Eighth Printing
Rainbow Books • P.O. Box 261129 • San Diego, CA 92196

#RB36191
ISBN 0-937282-33-2

CONTENTS

Introduction

Children learn best and remember more when they can see and visualize what they are taught. In fact, we learn 83 percent by sight and only 12 percent by hearing and touch together. But when hearing, touch *and* sight are combined, learning is much easier and effective.

Bulletin boards are a very effective way to teach children important biblical concepts so they will remember them. Because bulletin boards are colorful and attention-getting, children are naturally drawn to them and to the lessons they teach.

Today, bulletin boards are far more than simply boards to hold announcements and notices. Think of bulletin boards as an important part of your Sunday school or Bible classroom for several reasons:

- Bulletin boards are simple, inexpensive and colorful ways to decorate your classroom and provide an attractive learning environment
- Bulletin boards help children visualize and remember important spiritual concepts far longer than just talking about them
- Bulletin boards stimulate discussion and learning of Bible truths
- Bulletin boards help focus children's attention on important concepts you want to teach
- Bulletin boards help relate spiritual concepts to the children's everyday lives
- Bulletin boards motivate children to think critically and creatively
- Bulletin boards display useful information, announcements and invitations
- Bulletin boards provide an opportunity for children and teachers to relate to each other as they construct bulletin boards together

This book (and the other three books in this series) contain 13 seasonal Bible bulletin boards which can help you effectively teach biblical concepts in the ways listed above. The patterns and instructions in this book make it easy to construct these delightful bulletin boards, and you won't need a lot of artistic talent to be successful either!

That's because each bulletin board includes complete instructions and suggestions for borders, background, materials and how to put everything together. Full-size patterns are also provided, as are large headline letters and three seasonal borders and corners. All patterns, letters and borders may be used right out of the book or traced, enlarged, reduced, duplicated or photocopied to make attractive classroom bulletin boards.

Each bulletin board also includes a suggested Bible Memory Verse for the class to learn together and ideas for using the bulletin board to teach important spiritual concepts. (The King James Version of the Bible is used unless noted otherwise.)

Each bulletin board is designed for use in Sunday schools. Many may also be used in kids clubs, Vacation Bible School, children's church, Christian schools or anywhere the Bible is taught. The age of children for which the bulletin board is appropriate is also noted.

So . . . turn your classroom into an exciting learning environment with the colorful seasonal Bible-teaching bulletin boards in this book!

How to Create Beautiful Bulletin Boards Using the Materials in this Book

Each of the 13 Bible-teaching bulletin boards for Fall in this book contains complete instructions and full-size patterns, lettering and seasonal borders and corners, plus instructions and suggestions for backgrounds and for putting the bulletin boards together. These four pages contain hints, tips and how-to's for using the materials in this book (and the other three books in this series) to create beautiful bulletin boards!

Backgrounds

Backgrounds are vital to the overall design of the bulletin board. In this book, simple suggestions are given for backgrounds for each bulletin board. Feel free to also experiment with materials you have on hand or which are readily available, such as:

- Textured fabrics: flannel, felt, burlap, cottons, cheesecloth
- Construction paper
- Crepe paper
- Wrapping paper, either solid color or with small print or design
- Colored tissue papers
- Newspapers
- Aluminum foil or foil-covered wrapping paper
- Brown paper bags crumpled and then flattened
- Bamboo or grass place mats or floor mats
- Colorful corrugated paper available from school supply stores
- Butcher paper
- Poster board on which figures can be permanently attached
- Maps
- Adhesive-backed plastic in a variety of colors or patterns

You may wish to choose one background which you can use for several bulletin boards during the season.

Borders

Borders make the bulletin board, so after your background is in place, it's time to frame your bulletin board with an attractive, colorful border. Three seasonal borders and matching corners are provided on pages 62 and 63 of this book for use with selected bulletin boards in this book. Other simple border suggestions are given with the remaining bulletin boards in this book.

To use the seasonal borders and corners on pages 62 and 63, duplicate enough copies of the border strip to frame the entire bulletin board. Also make four copies of the matching corner. (Corners can also be used by themselves, or with strips of construction paper forming the border.)

You may duplicate the border and corner on white paper and have the children color the border with markers. (Markers give brighter colors than crayons, so are preferable for all bulletin board work), or you may wish to reproduce the border and corner onto colored paper. (See "Duplicating Patterns and Lettering" below.)

Overlap the border strips slightly and glue or tape the sections together. Use double faced tape to attach the border and corners directly to the frame of the bulletin board or staple the border and corners to the edge of the bulletin board just inside the frame. Roll the border to store for future use.

Attractive borders can also be made with the following materials attached to the frame of the bulletin board:

- Artificial flowers, real or artificial leaves, nature items
- Rope or twine
- Braided yarn
- Wide gift-wrap ribbon
- Purchased corrugated borders available from school supply stores
- Strips of twisted crepe paper 3/4 inch wide
- Strips of construction paper cut in attractive shapes, such as scallops, zig-zags, fringes, etc.

Making Bulletin Boards Three-Dimensional

Although bulletin boards are normally flat, there are many imaginative ways you can add a three-dimensional effect to your bulletin boards. Many of the bulletin boards in this book already include ideas for three-dimensional effects, but here are more you may like to try:

- Put a cork, thick piece of cardboard, or styrofoam behind figures or lettering
- Attach large figures to the bulletin board by curving them slightly outward from the board
- Glue or attach three-dimensional or textured objects such as cotton balls, small pieces of wood, twigs, nature items, feathers, yarn, children's toys, small clothing objects (like scarves and mittens), balloons, artificial flowers or leaves, chenille wire, fabrics and burlap, bamboo or woven place mats, corrugated paper, sandpaper, crumpled aluminum foil or grocery bags, rope, drinking straws, and such
- Use artificial spray snow for a winter scene
- "Stuff" figures by putting crumpled newspaper or paper towels behind the figures before attaching to the bulletin board
- Flowers can be made from individual sections cut from egg cartons
- Heavy objects (such as a small tree branch or a toy) may be mounted securely in the following way: Cut two or more strips of bias binding tape or ribbon (available from fabric stories). Securely staple one end of the bias tape to the bulletin board, place around the item to be mounted and staple the other end (above the object) to the bulletin board so the object hangs securely on the bias tape straps.

Lettering

Each bulletin board in this book includes full-sized lettering which is to be used with the full-size patterns to create your bulletin board. To use the lettering, you may do the following:

- Cut the lettering out of any paper. Place the page(s) of lettering from this book over the sheet(s) of paper out of which you want to cut the letters. Cut through both sheets, using scissors or a craft knife. Mount letters individually on the bulletin board.
- Duplicate the lettering onto white paper and color in the letters with markers.
- Duplicate the lettering onto white or colored construction paper or copy machine paper. Cut the words apart and mount each word on the bulletin board in strip form.
- Trace the lettering onto paper of any color using colored markers. Cut out individual letters or cut apart words and use in strip form.
- Cut individual letters out of two colors of paper at once. When mounting letters on the bulletin board, lay one color on top of the other and offset the bottom letter slightly so it creates a shadow effect.

Attractive lettering can also be made by cutting letters out of wallpaper, fabrics, felt, adhesive-backed plastic in various colors or patterns, wrapping paper, grocery bags which have been crumpled and then flattened, old newspapers and other materials. For a professional look, outline letters with a dark marker for a neat edge and good contrast. Always try to use dark colors for lettering.

Textures can be used for lettering also, either by cutting the letters out of textured materials or by gluing on glitter, sequins, straw, twigs, yarn, rope, lace, craft or ice cream sticks, chenille wire or other materials.

To mount letters flat, staple to the board, use double-sided tape or roll a small piece of tape to make it double-sided. Always put the tape under the letter so it does not show.

Position letters either in a straight line or in a curved or staggered arrangement. Space letters attractively.

Duplicating Patterns and Lettering

All patterns, lettering, borders and corners in this book may be used right out of the book or traced, enlarged, reduced, duplicated or photocopied to make attractive classroom bulletin boards.

The easiest way to duplicate the materials in this book is to use a copy machine to simply copy the patterns, lettering or borders onto white or colored copy machine paper. (Copy machine paper is available in a wide variety of colors ranging from pastel colors to very bright colors.) For a very nominal price you can copy onto these colored papers at most copy centers. Construction paper also works in some copy machines.

You can also trace materials in this book onto white or colored paper by holding the page you wish to trace up to a window or by using carbon paper.

You can also color the materials from this book with markers.

The easiest way to reduce or enlarge materials is to use a copy machine which enlarges or reduces, available at most copy centers also.

You can also trace the items you wish to enlarge onto a overhead projector transparency, project the transparency onto a sheet of paper on a wall, adjusting the image to the size you wish, and trace the image onto the white or colored paper. An opaque projector can also be used to enlarge patterns without having to trace them onto transparency material.

Mounting Materials on Your Bulletin Board

It is important that all materials stay securely on your bulletin board until you wish to take them down. Stapling materials directly to the bulletin board is the most secure method of mounting most materials and the staples are virtually unnoticeable. Be sure to have a staple puller handy to help prevent frustration and broken fingernails. Staples are also much better for bulletin boards for small children as it is quite difficult to pull a staple out of the bulletin board, unlike pins and tacks. Be sure no loose staples are left on the floor after you finish putting up the bulletin board.

Pins can be used if you wish to support the materials rather than make holes. Double-faced tape, or tape rolled to make it double faced is also effective. For heavier materials, use carpet tape or packing tape.

How to Make Your Bulletin Boards Durable and Reusable

Cover both sides of your bulletin board figures with clear adhesive-backed plastic. Cut around the figures, leaving a 1/4 inch edge of plastic. (If one figure is made up of several parts, put the parts together before covering with the plastic.) You can also glue figures to colored construction paper and cut around the figure, leaving a narrow border of construction paper.

Teaching with the Bulletin Boards

Each of the bulletin boards in this book includes a suggested Bible Memory Verse and teaching tips to help you use the bulletin boards to teach important biblical concepts to your students.

In addition, children 8 years and older enjoy helping with the construction of the bulletin boards and are delighted to help cut, color, glue and staple. This provides a great opportunity for the message of the board to "soak in" while the children and teacher get to know each other better as they work together. The more the children are involved in constructing the bulletin boards, the better and more effective their learning will be.

Appropriate for ages 7 to 12

Background and Border:

Cover board with tan or light brown corrugated paper or fabric. Duplicate the Harvest border and corner from pages 62 and 63 onto colored paper or color with markers.

Materials and Instructions:

Cut turkey's head from page 13 out of tan or light brown paper and turkey's body from page 12 out of dark brown paper. Staple to board, overlapping body over head slightly. Add feet from page 12 cut out of orange paper. Glue on large movable eyes, red wattle and orange beak.

Cut several feathers from various colors of construction paper using pattern on page 13. Write on each feather one thing for which we are to be thankful. Staple into place on board.

Cut lettering from page 11 out of red paper or duplicate the lettering onto orange or goldenrod paper and use in strip form.

Teaching with this Bulletin Board:

Learn the Bible Memory Verse together. Give one feather to each child. Let each child say the verse, naming one thing for which he is thankful, "We give Thee thanks, O Lord God, for. . ." Then each child may write the thing for which they are thankful on the feather and staple his or her feather in place on the board.

Suggested Bible Memory Verse:

"We give Thee thanks, O Lord God." — Revelation 11:17

Give
Thanks for
All Things

Turkey's body:
Cut out of dark brown paper.

Turkey's feet:
Cut out of
orange paper.

12

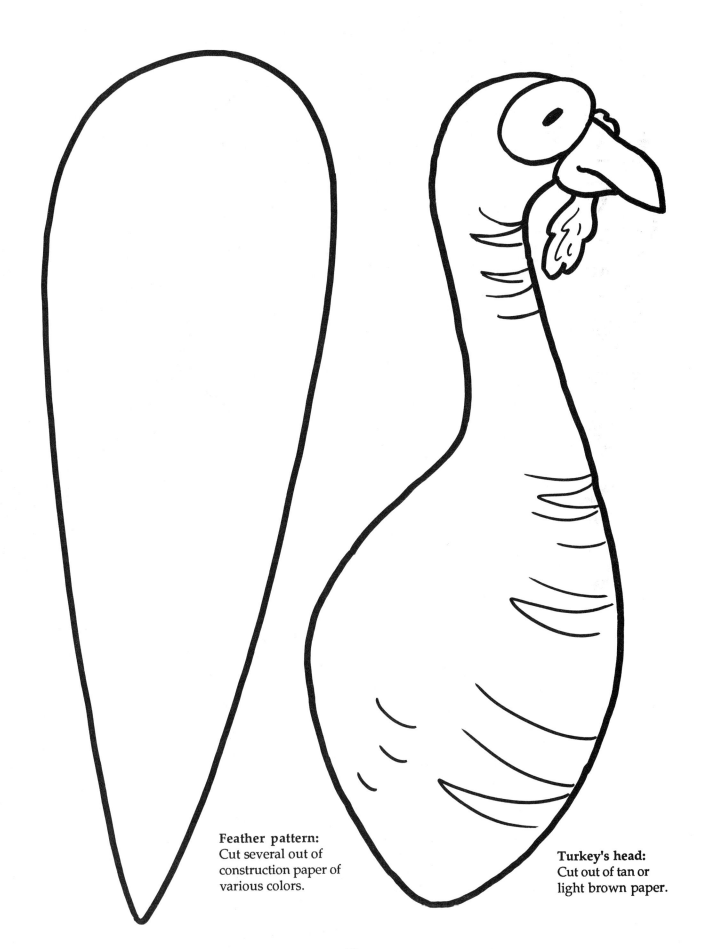

Feather pattern:
Cut several out of
construction paper of
various colors.

Turkey's head:
Cut out of tan or
light brown paper.

13

Appropriate for ages 4 to 10

Background and Border:

Cover bulletin board with peach or light orange paper or fabric. Duplicate the Harvest border and corner from pages 62 and 63 onto colored paper or color with markers.

Materials and Instructions:

Duplicate boy's and girl's heads and arms (with closed hands); boy's feet, shirt and pants; and girl's blouse, skirt and legs from pages 59-61. Cut clothing out of fabric. Put ribbon bow in girl's hair. Assemble body and clothing to form figures and attach to board. Cut apron out of lace fabric. Staple into bag shape behind girl's hands. Place a few real nuts into apron. Glue or tape a few real nuts to the board also.

Cut leaves out of red, brown, gold and orange felt and staple into place. Or use real fall leaves which have been polished with floor wax to make them shiny and durable.

From page 17, duplicate the pumpkin onto orange paper and the squirrel onto rust-colored paper. Staple into place.

Duplicate the basket from page 16 two times onto tan or light brown paper. Staple one basket into a rounded shape on the board. (Or make the baskets using the instructions for the "Harvest the Fruit of the Spirit" bulletin board on pages 55 - 58.) Duplicate several apples from page 16 and extend above the rim. Place the second basket in the boy's hands and fill with more apples from page 16.

Cut lettering from page 15 out of gold construction paper or duplicate onto goldenrod paper and use in strip form.

Teaching with this Bulletin Board:

Learn the Bible Memory Verse together. Talk about why God made fall and some of the things that happen during fall. Let each child name one thing about fall for which they are thankful.

Suggested Bible Memory Verse:

"Lord, . . . You created all things." — Revelation 4:11 NIV

14

Thank

God

You

Fall

For

Apples: Duplicate several onto red and green paper.

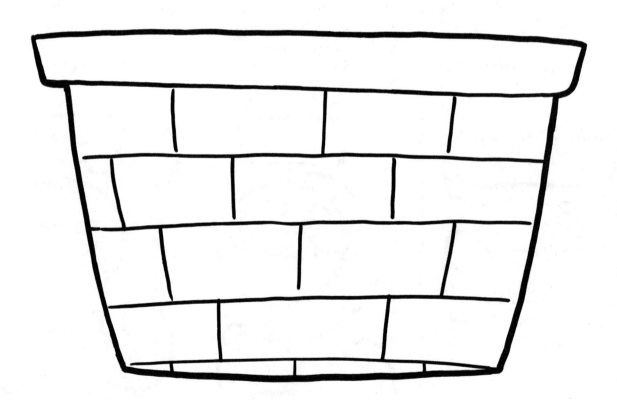

Basket: Duplicate two times onto
tan or light brown paper.

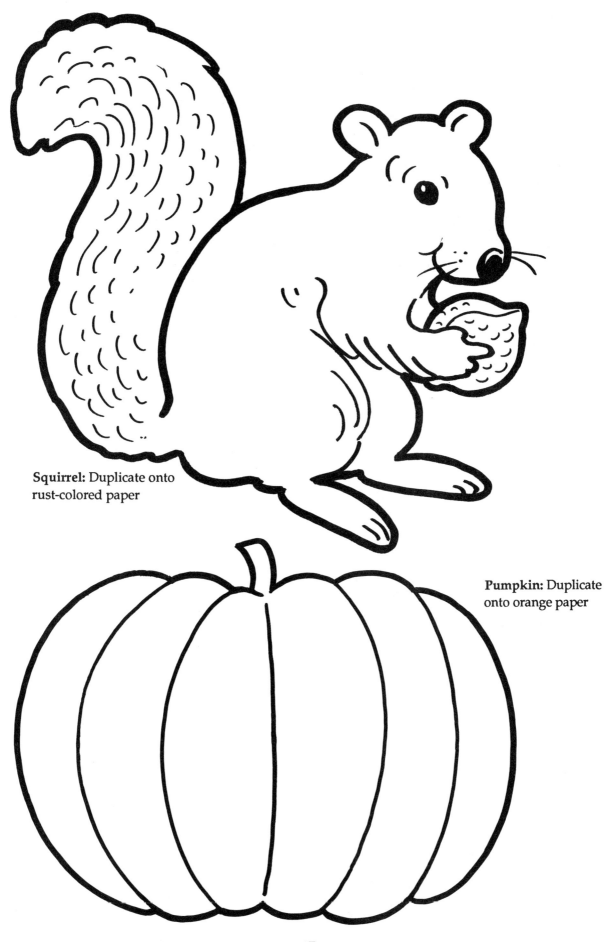

Squirrel: Duplicate onto rust-colored paper

Pumpkin: Duplicate onto orange paper

Appropriate for ages 6 to 11

Background and Border:

Cover top two-thirds of board with light blue paper or fabric and cover lower one-third of board with green paper. Fringe strips of green paper and put along upper edge of green area to represent grass. Use the Fall Leaves border and corner from pages 62 and 63 duplicated onto colored paper or color with markers, or cut a green construction paper border.

Materials and Instructions:

Sketch a tree onto brown or grey poster board and cut out. Or crumple a large grocery bag, flatten out and cut out tree. Draw in bark and details with a black marker. Cut a large black "hole" out of construction paper and glue to the trunk of the tree. Staple tree to board.

Duplicate the raccoons from page 19 onto brown, grey, tan and white paper. (Be sure raccoons contrast with the color of the tree.) Color with markers. Position on the tree.

The lettering from pages 20 and 21 may be duplicated onto gold or orange paper or individual letters may be cut out of orange construction paper. Staple into position on the board.

Teaching with this Bulletin Board:

Talk about why it is important for Christians to attend Sunday school. Talk about some of the things we learn in Sunday school. Encourage the children to invite their friends. Learn the Bible Memory Verse together.

This bulletin board can also be used to reward attendance. Make a small raccoon for each child. At the beginning of class each week, the child may put his raccoon on the tree.

Suggested Bible Memory Verse:

"I will come into Thy house." — Psalm 5:7

Raccoons:
Cut several out of brown, grey, tan and white paper. Color with markers.

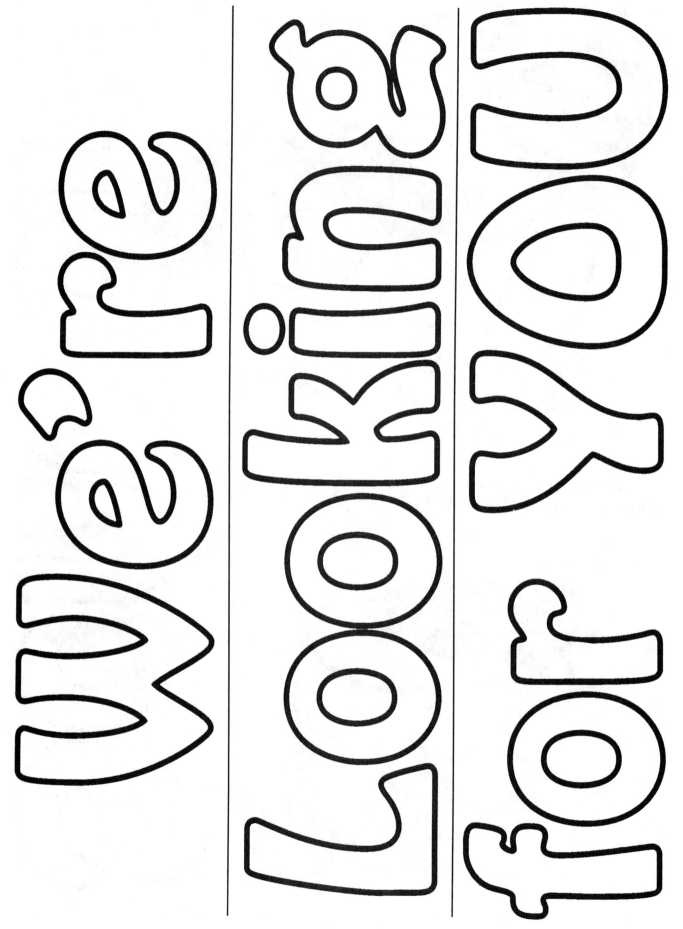

We're
Looking
for YOU

In Sunday School

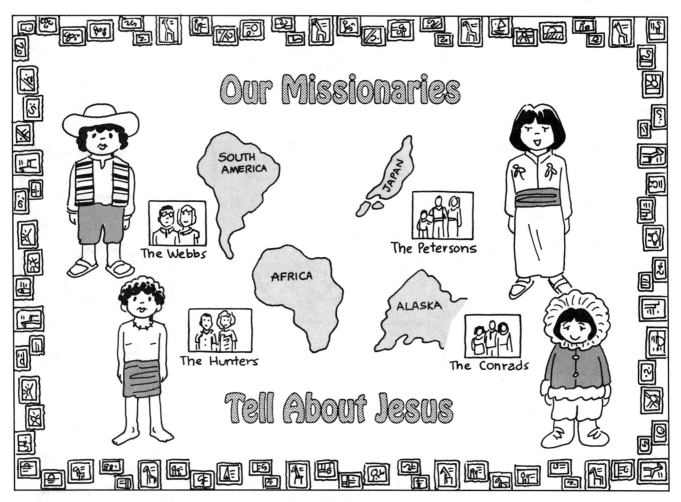

Appropriate for ages 7 to 12

Background and Border:

Cover bulletin board with yellow paper or fabric. Cut strips of dark blue construction paper for border. Glue foreign postage stamps to the strips and mount the strips on the bulletin board.

Materials and Instructions:

Duplicate figures of children from pages 24 and 25 onto colored paper or color with markers. If desired, glue on fabric and fake fur for clothing.

Out of various colors of construction paper cut simple outline maps of countries in which your church has missionaries serving. Staple to board. Near the maps, mount photos of the missionaries or their activities. Mount the figures of children nearby also.

Duplicate lettering from page 23 onto blue paper. Arrange on board as shown in illustration above.

Teaching with this Bulletin Board:

Use this bulletin board to make children aware of missionary work and the need to support missionaries through giving and prayer. Learn the Bible Memory Verse together. Talk about what it means to "preach the Gospel." Make sure the children understand that they too can "preach the Gospel" by telling others about Jesus right where they are.

Talk about what missionaries do to tell about Jesus (operate hospitals, teach children, hold church services, etc.). Introduce the children to the missionaries shown on the board by telling about their work, family members and location. Then pray for each missionary family.

Suggested Bible Memory Verse:

"Go ye into all the world, and preach the gospel." — Mark 16:15

Tell

Our

Missionaries

About Jesus

South American child   Eskimo child

African child

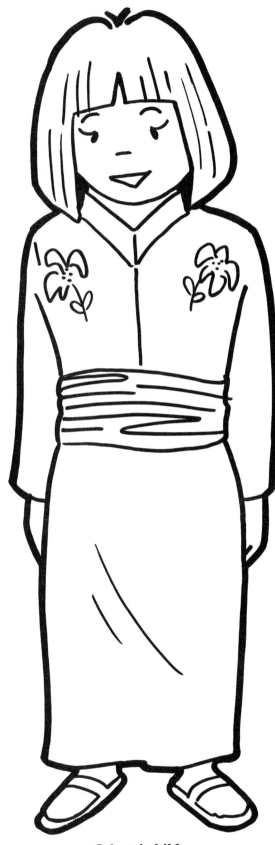

Oriental child

Appropriate for ages 8 to 12

Background and Border:

Cover board with blue paper, fabric or wrapping paper. Use a corrugated border which compliments the background and clothing of the children, or duplicate and color the School Times border and corner from pages 62 and 63.

Materials and Instructions:

Enlarge the boy's and girl's heads from page 59 to the desired size for your board. Glue on yarn hair, if desired, and add a bow or barrettes in the girl's hair. Enlarge and trace the boy's shirt from page 60 onto white paper two times. Color in red stripes. Staple heads and shirts to the board.

Form three-dimensional megaphones out of bright yellow construction paper cut in a quarter-circle shape. Roll into megaphone shape and staple to the bulletin board. Tape children's lower arms (enlarged from page 59) to the megaphones.

Duplicate "The Word is Out" lettering from page 27 onto bright yellow construction paper and

cut out. Or duplicate onto colored paper and use in strip form. Staple to the board.

Duplicate "Jesus Loves You!" lettering twice and staple just outside the wide end of the megaphone. For the best effect, cut individual letters out of red construction paper or duplicate onto colored paper and use in strip form. If desired, you may substitute other wording.

Teaching with this Bulletin Board:

Discuss why it is important for us to tell others about Jesus, and ways the children can do this. You may want to show the children how to lead someone to Christ, with one child giving the plan of salvation and another child playing the person receiving Christ. (Be sure to offer an opportunity for children who've not received Jesus to do so.) Learn the Bible Memory Verse .

Suggested Bible Memory Verse:

"I will declare Thy greatness." —Psalm 145:6

The Word

is Out!

Jesus Loves You!

Store Your Treasures in Heaven

Appropriate for ages 10 to 12

Background and Border:

Cover board with light blue paper or fabric. Duplicate and color the Fall Leaves border and corner from pages 62-63, or use real fall leaves which have been waxed with floor polish to make them shiny and durable.

Materials and Instructions:

Cut tree shape out of brown poster board or a grocery bag crumpled and then flattened. Cut large black "hole" out of construction paper and glue on tree trunk. Glue or tape actual nuts in the squirrel's "hole" or cut nuts out of tan or orange paper. Staple tree to bulletin board.

Duplicate squirrel from page 29 onto rust construction paper and staple into place on tree branch.

Place an actual nut in squirrel's paws.

Cut lettering from page 30 out of orange construction paper or duplicate onto colored paper and use in strip form.

Teaching with this Bulletin Board:

Discuss and learn the Bible Memory Verse. Talk about what it means to "store up treasures in heaven." What are some treasures we can store up in heaven? Why does the Bible say "where your treasure is, there your heart will be also?" What does this mean?

Suggested Bible Memory Verse:

"Store up for yourselves treasures in heaven, . . . For where your treasure is, there your heart will be also." — Matthew 6:20-21 NIV

Squirrel:
Cut out of rust
construction paper.

Store Your Treasures in Heaven

Appropriate for ages 6 to 12

Background and Border:

Cover board with beige burlap or rough-textured fabric. Duplicate the Fall Leaves border and corner from pages 62 and 63 onto colored paper or color with markers. You could substitute a green corrugated or construction paper border, if desired.

Materials and Instructions:

Duplicate the owl from pages 32 and 33 onto brown construction paper. Glue on an orange beak. Cut large white ovals for eyes and glue on black pupils. Glue on real feathers or feathers cut from construction paper. Staple to board, putting some crumpled newspapers behind the owl to give it a slightly stuffed, three-dimensional effect. Cut owl's feet out of gold construction paper. Position the feet on a real tree branch. Cut green construction paper leaves and glue or tape to the branch.

Cut lettering from pages 34 and 35 out of green construction paper or duplicate onto colored paper and use in strip form.

Teaching with this Bulletin Board:

Discuss why it is important to attend Sunday school each week. What are some of the important things we learn and do in Sunday school? Learn the Bible Memory Verse together.

Suggested Bible Memory Verse:

"Let us go into the house of the Lord." — Psalm 122:1

Owl's feet:
Cut out of gold paper.

Owl:
Cut out of brown paper. Glue on real feathers or feathers cut out of construction paper.

Hoo! Hoo! We Want

You in

Sunday

School

Appropriate for ages 7 to 11

Background and Border:

Duplicate the School Time border and corner from pages 62 and 63 onto colored paper or color with markers. Cover board with a tiny calico print fabric or solid paper or fabric in an autumn color.

Materials and Instructions:

Duplicate Boy and Girl Figures and Clothing from pages 59 - 61. Cut some or all of clothing out of actual fabric. Use denim for the boy's pants, striped fabric for his shirt, and plaid fabric for the girl's skirt and blouse. Add a bit of lace for the collar and put a bow in the girl's hair. Duplicate the backpack and stack of books from page 37 for the children to carry.

Make several large books from page 37 by cutting them out of various colors of construction paper or copy them onto colored copy machine paper. Cut out.

Arrange lettering duplicated from pages 38 and 39. The lettering will be very attractive if cut out of construction paper which compliments the colors in the background and children's clothing. Or cut the letters out of plaid wrapping paper and outline each letter with a dark marking pen.

Teaching with this Bulletin Board:

Discuss what it means to live for Jesus. Let the children name things they can do at school which are pleasing to Jesus. Let each child write one thing on a book duplicated from page 37. They may also decorate or color the books if desired. Staple books to the board. Learn the Bible Memory Verse together and talk about what it means to "study to show thyself approved unto God."

Suggested Bible Memory Verse:

"Study to show thyself approved unto God." — II Timothy 2:15

Large book:
Duplicate onto colored paper

**Backpack for
boy to carry**

Books for girl to carry

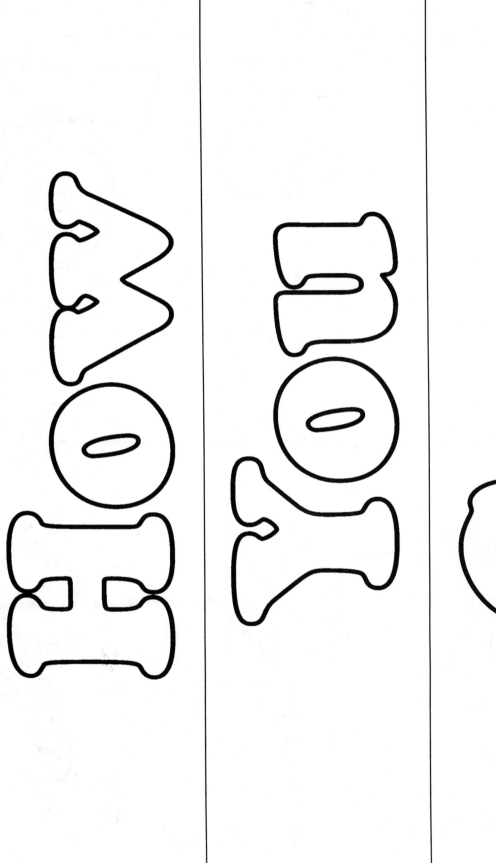

How You Can

38

Live for Jesus at school

Appropriate for ages 3 to 11

Background and Border:

Cover board with tan or beige burlap or other rough-textured fabric. Use colorful corrugated border or cut scolloped strips of construction paper.

Materials and Instructions:

Make railroad track by cutting black construction paper strips with square notches as shown above. Staple to board. Duplicate as many train cars from page 43 as desired onto various colors of construction paper. Duplicate engine from page 42 onto red paper. Glue on yellow or gold smoke stack and brown cow catcher. Cut colorful circles out of construction paper and glue on engine and cars for wheels. Staple to board.

Make engineer out of chenille wire. Tie a scrap of red fabric around his neck and cut a cap out of blue construction paper or fabric.

Cut smoke cloud out of grey poster board or large piece of construction paper. Trace "All Aboard" lettering from page 41 onto smoke with black marker or cut out individual letters and glue

in place. Staple cloud to board.

Cut remainder of lettering from page 41 out of blue construction paper (or other complimentary color) or duplicate the lettering onto colored paper and use in strip form.

Teaching with this Bulletin Board:

Use this Bulletin Board to encourage the children to become a regular part of your Sunday school class and to invite their friends to Sunday school also. Learn the Bible Memory Verse together. Talk about why we are to love God's house and the importance of Sunday school.

If desired, children's pictures can be mounted in the windows of the train cars as they enroll in your Sunday school. For younger children, animals could be cut out of construction paper. As each child enrolls, he places an animal with his name in the train car.

Suggested Bible Memory Verse:

"Lord, I have loved. . . Thy house." — Psalm 26:8

all Aboard

Aboard...

Sunday

Join

School our

41

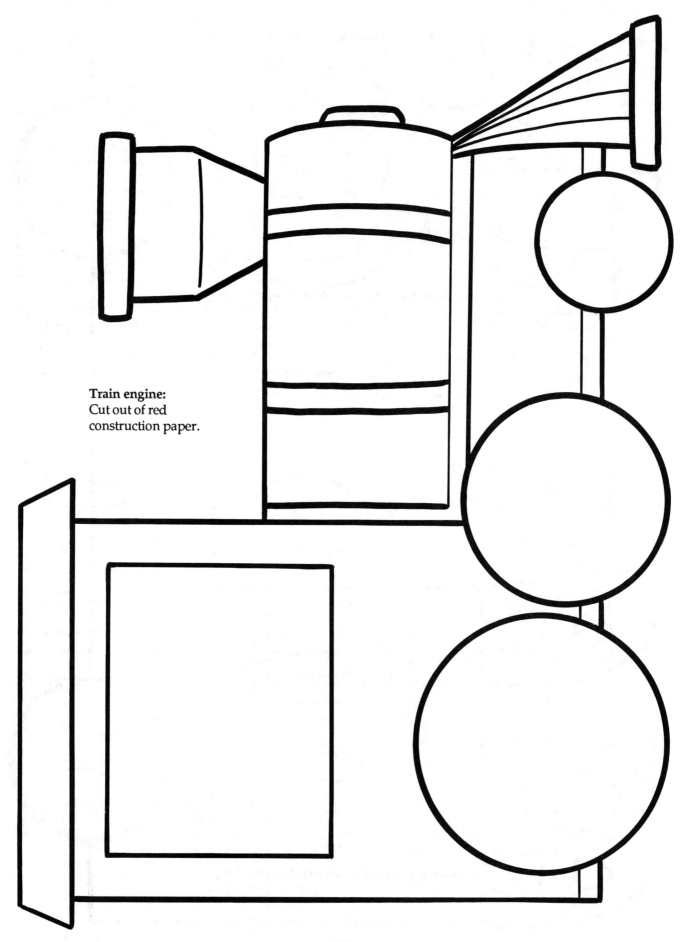

Train engine:
Cut out of red
construction paper.

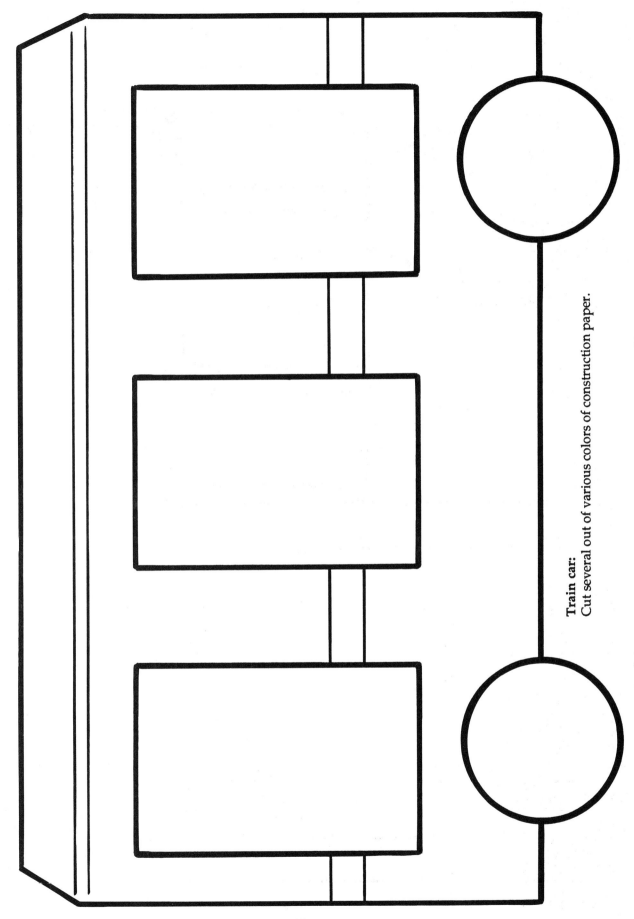

Train car:
Cut several out of various colors of construction paper.

Appropriate for ages 2 to 6

Background and Border:

Cover bulletin board with burlap or other rough-textured material. Use colorful orange or red corrugated border for more texture.

Materials and Instructions:

Cut large tree trunk out of brown construction paper or sandpaper. Staple to board. Cut orange, red, gold and brown leaves from felt. Place the leaves in a plastic bag with some potpourri or put in a few drops of perfume or after shave. Allow the scent to penetrate the leaves. Staple some leaves onto the tree and some around the bottom of the tree. (Use only one staple so the leaves hang loosely.)

Mount a small stuffed toy animal at the foot of the tree. Glue cotton balls or cotton batting to the board to create clouds.

Shape flower stems and leaves from chenille wire and glue to the board. Glue gumdrops to small circles of poster board to form flowers. Staple circles to the board.

Cut lettering from page 45 out of orange paper or duplicate and use in strip form.

Teaching with this Bulletin Board:

This bulletin board uses all the children's senses to experience God's creations. (Since you don't want to encourage the children to taste the gumdrops on the board, provide gumdrops for snacking. See who can make the prettiest gumdrop flower before eating their candy.)

Talk to the children about the wonderful world God created and point out the different things God made represented on the bulletin board (animals, flowers, trees, clouds). Allow the children to touch the different textures. Ask the children to name one of God's creation they enjoy. Learn the Bible Memory Verse together. Then lead the children in saying prayers of thanksgiving to God. "Thank You, God for trees. Thank You, God for clouds."

Suggested Bible Memory Verse:

"God created the heaven and the earth." —Genesis 1:1

I Enjoy

God's

World

Appropriate for ages 8 to 11

Background and Border:

Cover bulletin board with tan or beige paper or fabric. Twist strips of dark brown and orange crepe paper together and attach to bulletin board frame to form border.

Materials and Instructions:

Duplicate boy's and girl's heads, lower arms and feet from pages 59 - 61. Cut boy's clown suit and hat from page 47 out of colorful paper or fabric. If desired, glue on colorful circles or round stickers. Glue a pompom on clown hat. If desired, color boy's face with markers to represent clown make-up. Mount all together to form clown.

Cut girl's princess dress from page 50 out of pastel fabric or paper. Glue on lace, glitter, sequins or other decorations as desired. Cut girl's crown out of gold paper or foil. Glue on sequins or glitter. Mount crown, girl's head, dress, feet and arms together to form figure.

Make the Bible by folding a large sheet of brown or black construction paper in half. Fold in half a sheet of white or beige construction paper which is slightly smaller than the brown or black sheet. Place on top of the brown or black sheet and staple both sheets to the bulletin board in the fold and at the corners, curving the paper out from the bulletin board to give a three-dimensional effect. Staple a piece of wide red ribbon or strip of fabric across the Bible pages as a bookmarker.

Cut lettering from pages 48 and 49 out of foil or shiny paper and outline with black marker or duplicate onto colored paper and use in strip form.

Teaching with this Bulletin Board:

Talk with the children about the attributes of the Bible: that it is trustworthy, inspired, truthful, and God's special message to us. Discuss the importance of Bible study and memorization. Learn the Bible Memory Verse.

Suggested Bible Memory Verse:

"Thy word is truth." — John 17:17

Boy's clown suit:
Use with boy's head, arms and feet from pages 59-60. Cut out of colored paper or fabric.

Boy's hat:
Cut out of colored paper or fabric. Glue on colorful circles and pompom.

47

The Bible Won't Trick

It's You... a Real Treat!

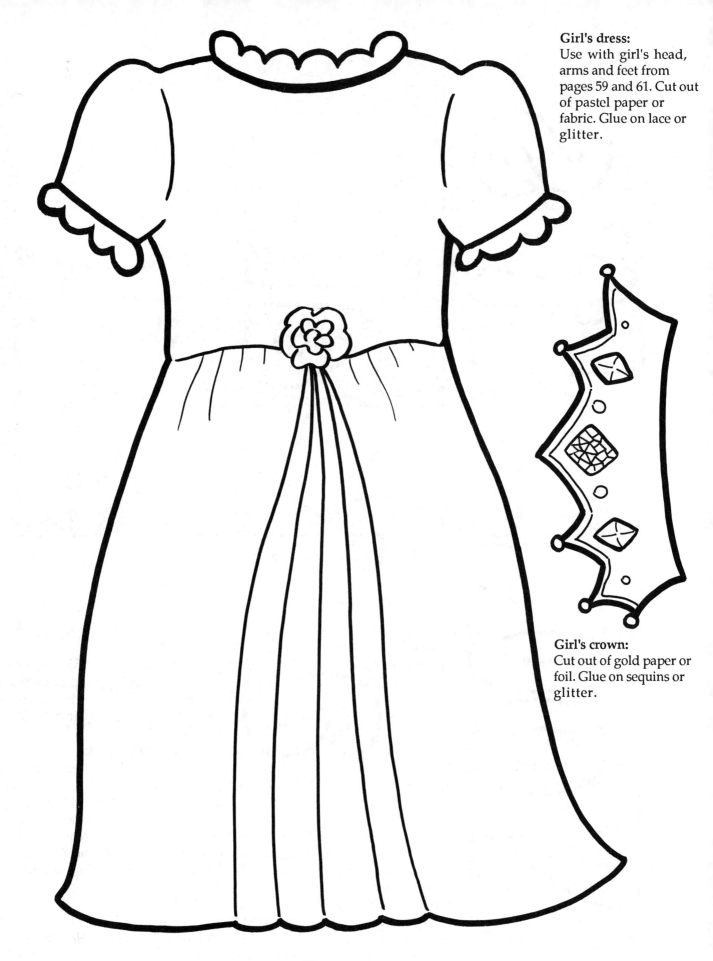

Girl's dress:
Use with girl's head, arms and feet from pages 59 and 61. Cut out of pastel paper or fabric. Glue on lace or glitter.

Girl's crown:
Cut out of gold paper or foil. Glue on sequins or glitter.

Give Thanks To the Lord for He is Good

Appropriate for ages 5 to 12

Background and Border:

Cover board with light blue fabric or paper. Duplicate Fall Leaves border and corner from pages 62 and 63 onto colored paper or color with markers. You could also make a border of real fall leaves which have been polished with floor wax to make them shiny and durable.

Materials and Instructions:

Cut table top of white construction paper or poster board. (Table top should be at least 14 inches long and shaped as shown above.) Cover with lace fabric or trim. Staple to board. Hang a strip of lace fabric or wide lace trim below table top to represent tablecloth. (Staple lace to board at the top only so the bottom hangs free.)

Duplicate the boy's and girl's bodies from page 54. Color with markers. Glue on lace for collar, and fabric for clothing, if desired. Duplicate and color boy's and girl's heads from page 59. Glue on yarn for hair, if desired, and add bow to girl's hair. Place heads and bodies together and staple to board

above the table top as shown.

Duplicate the turkey from page 54 onto white paper and color with markers. Staple into place on the table.

Cut lettering from pages 52 and 53 out of construction paper in fall colors which compliment the colors in the border. You may also duplicate the lettering onto colored paper and use in strip form.

Teaching with this Bulletin Board:

Learn the Bible Memory Verse together. Talk about ways in which God is good to us. Discuss Thanksgiving and why we celebrate God's goodness in this way. Ask each child to name something for which he or she is thankful. Then lead each child in a short sentence prayer, "Thank You, God for my puppy." "Thank You, God for my friend, Aimee."

Suggested Bible Memory Verse:

"O give thanks unto the Lord; for He is good." — Psalm 136:1

Give

Thanks

To the

52

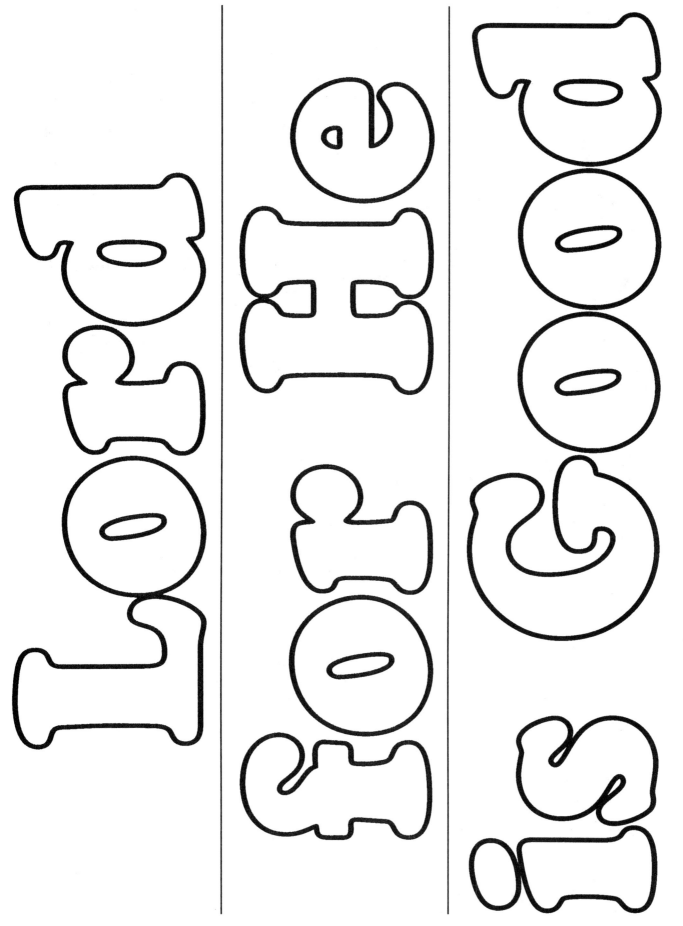

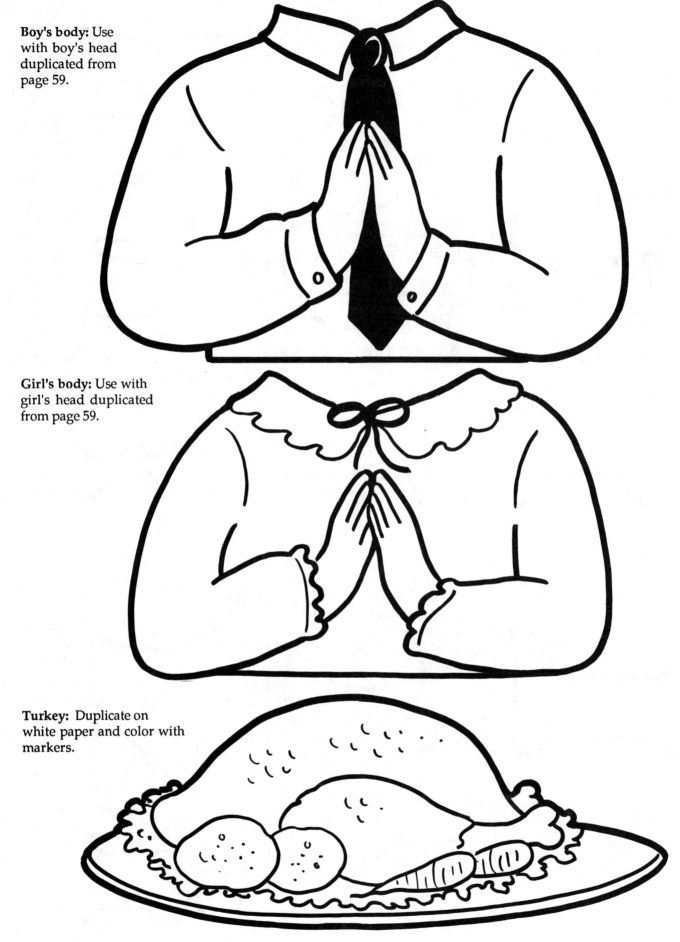

Boy's body: Use with boy's head duplicated from page 59.

Girl's body: Use with girl's head duplicated from page 59.

Turkey: Duplicate on white paper and color with markers.

54

Harvest the Fruit of the Spirit

Appropriate for ages 9 to 12

Background and Border:

Cover top two-thirds of board with light blue paper or fabric. Cover bottom one-third of board with green paper or fabric. If using paper and if desired, fringe the upper edge of the green paper to represent grass. Duplicate and color the Harvest border and corner from pages 62 and 63.

Materials and Instructions:

Form the bushel basket by cutting a basket shape out of tan poster board. Make slits as shown in illustration on page 57 and weave strips of brown construction paper through the slits. Glue the ends of the strips and allow to dry.

Staple the basket to the board while curving it slightly to create a three-dimensional effect.

Duplicate nine of the fruit shapes from pages 56 and 57. Write one of the fruits of the Spirit from Galatians 5:22 on each fruit shape. Staple to the board, arranging the fruit in and around the basket.

Cut lettering from page 58 out of blue construction paper or duplicate the lettering onto colored paper and use in strip form.

Teaching with this Bulletin Board:

Talk with the children about the fruits of the Spirit and how to dedicate their lives to the Lord completely. Discuss each fruit individually as the children may not know the meaning of each fruit. Give one fruit shape to each of nine children. As you say the Bible Memory Verse together, have each child put his fruit on the bulletin board with a pin. (Fruits can be stapled in place later.)

Suggested Bible Memory Verse:

"The fruit of the Spirit is love, joy, peace, patience, kindness, goodness, faithfulness, gentleness and self-control." — Galatians 5:22 NIV

Banana:
Cut out of
yellow paper.

Apple:
Cut out of red paper.

56

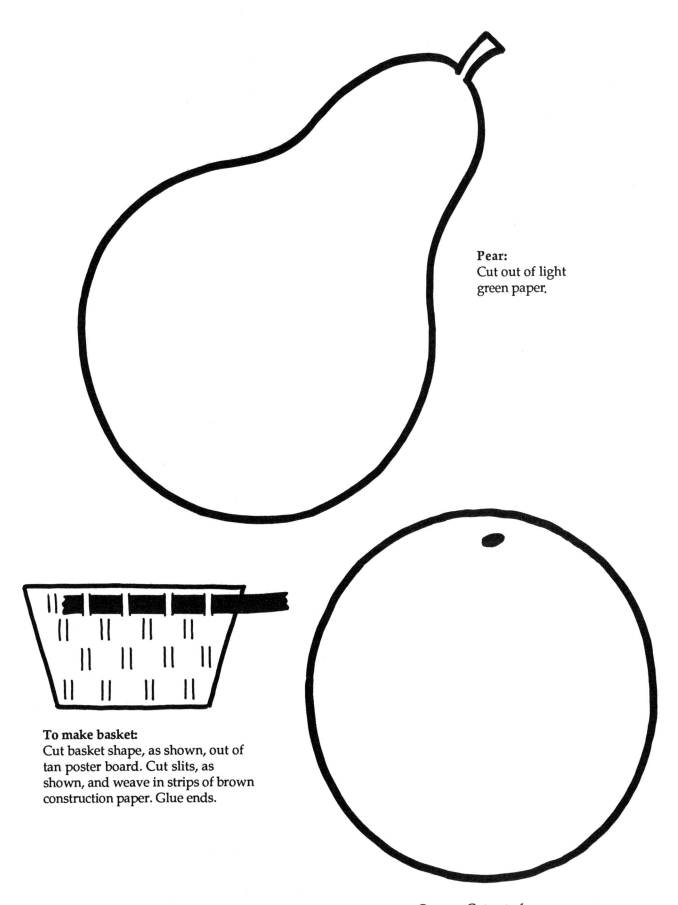

Pear:
Cut out of light green paper.

To make basket:
Cut basket shape, as shown, out of tan poster board. Cut slits, as shown, and weave in strips of brown construction paper. Glue ends.

Orange: Cut out of orange paper.

Harvest the

Fruit of

the Spirit

Lower arms with open hands

Boy's head

How to make
Boy and Girl Figures:

Clothing and body parts are provided on these pages to create large-size boy and girl figures to use on several bulletin boards.

To easily make these figures, copy the boy's and girl's heads and arms onto pink, beige, tan or light brown copy machine paper (depending on nationality you want to create). Color in features with markers. Glue on yarn for hair. Put a bow in the girl's hair and glue on movable eyes, if desired.

Copy boy's feet and girl's legs onto white paper and color in shoes and stockings with markers.

Clothing can be made in several ways:
1. Duplicate clothing onto copy machine paper of various colors.
2. Trace clothing onto construction paper and cut out.
3. Copy clothing onto white paper. Cut clothing shapes out of fabric and glue to the white paper. Glue on trims, small buttons and other items to add a three dimensional effect.

To make the figures durable and reusable, glue the clothing and body parts together onto a large sheet of construction paper or poster board. After glue dries cut out around the entire figures and attach to the bulletin board.

Girl's head

Lower arms with closed hands

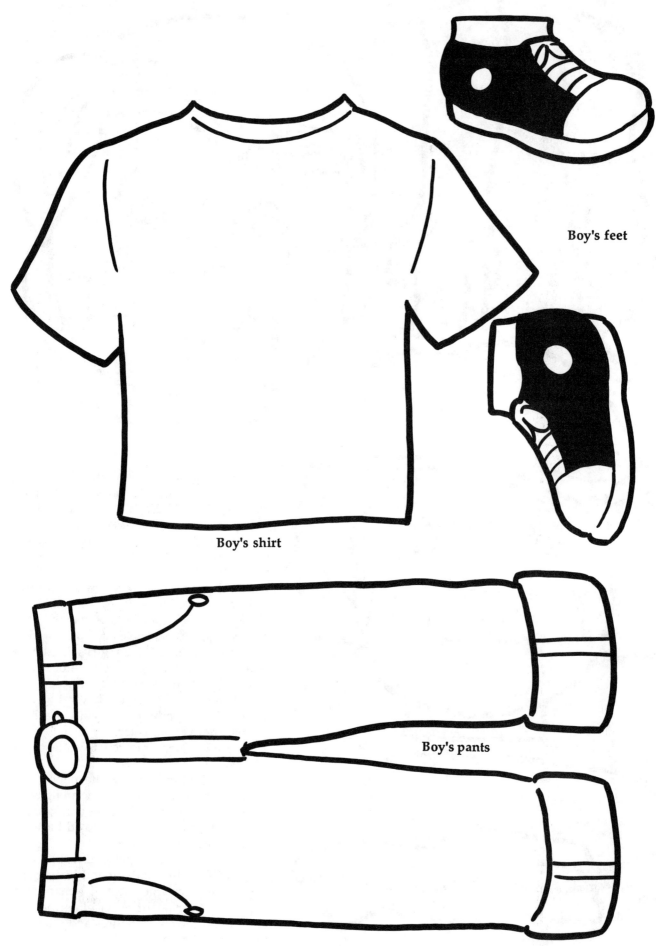

Boy's feet

Boy's shirt

Boy's pants

60

Girl's blouse

Girl's legs

Girl's skirt

School Time Corner

Fall Leaves Corner

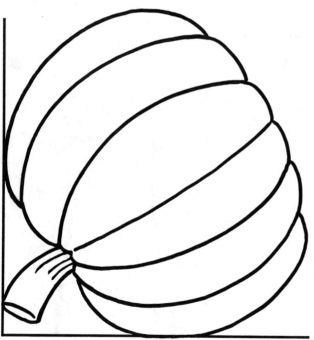

Harvest Corner

How to Use Fall Borders and Corners

Choose the border you wish to use. Duplicate enough copies of that border strip to cover the entire frame of your bulletin board. In addition, make four copies of the matching corner.

You may duplicate the borders and corners onto white paper and color in the borders with markers. (The children will enjoy helping you do this.)

Or you may wish to duplicate the borders and corners onto colored copy machine paper or construction paper which compliments the background colors in the bulletin board.

Overlap the border strips slightly and glue or tape the sections together. Roll the border to store for future use.

School Time Border

Fall Leaves Border

Harvest Border